DIFFICULT TO SURVIVE WELL

MOMINUL AMIN

ISBN 979-888521184-0

This book has been published with all efforts taken to make the material error-free after the consent of the author. However, the author and the publisher do not assume and hereby disclaim any liability to any party for any loss, damage, or disruption caused by errors or omissions, whether such errors or omissions result from negligence, accident, or any other cause.

While every effort has been made to avoid any mistake or omission, this publication is being sold on the condition and understanding that neither the author nor the publishers or printers would be liable in any manner to any person by reason of any mistake or omission in this publication or for any action taken or omitted to be taken or advice rendered or accepted on the basis of this work. For any defect in printing or binding the publishers will be liable only to replace the defective copy by another copy of this work then available.

My PARENTS

Contents

Foreword

We have tried our best to present the book to you properly.However, if you find any errors in this book,please let us know by mail and we will try tocorrect it as soon as possible.

Preface

Even after having everything for a long time in life.we don,t fell god. in fact, you don't neetd these things to be good,you need some good people.

Acknowledgements

First of all I would like to thank my parents and family for bringing me into this world. I am also forever grateful to the people who always look at me with respect and love. I will always be grateful to the people who have always helped me. I also pray for all those people who have kept themselves well in the midst of so much suffering or have tried to keep themselves well. Let us all take an oath to be good and to be good together.

Abaout Author

MOMINUL AMIN

Book writter, motivational speaker, ethical hacker, you tuber,app creater, website developer etc

Date of birth=12/12/2001

ABAOUT AUTHOR

make your own old

Prologue

take care

Some Of The Author's Words

Why did I write the book? Why should the book be read? I will try to answer these questions. How would I feel if I didn't share some things with you? So I am sharing the words with you. In fact, I want you to listen to these words. At first the name of the book is why I told the story in a beautiful way below that is why I gave the name of the book. So at first I thought for several days I would write a book. At first I was thinking of writing about several topics. Ever thought I would write a romantic story. But again I think what a romantic story I really should write. Then I thought maybe I should write a book on ethical hacking. I also wrote it like 10 pages. Then it was no longer written. I spend about four to five months writing like this. Then one night I decided to write a new book. Which will come in handy for all of us. And from that I wrote 'Is it very difficult to be good?'. When I first started writing, I thought I would write in 200 to 300 pages. But when I sat down to write, after writing 10 pages, it seemed that I had written all the ideas in my head in 10 pages. Then I thought that this book might not be written like other books. Then I was very worried about it. Because I haven't been able to write for a long time. Then decide to write a book before stopping all work. And I immediately decided that I would have to take a break from all my phones and social media for a whole few days. And I switched off all my phones. Then for about 14 days I was separated from the people of the whole world. I was confined to a house. In between, I read books by more than a hundred different authors. I wonder what I did in just 14 days. Maybe if someone gave me 365 days, maybe that's all I have

I could never finish reading a book. Maybe I managed to be firm. My parents are the ones who are most surprised to see me. He always saw me busy with the phone. But all of a sudden I was studying for 14 to 15 hours and to them it was one of the most amazing things they saw. I wondered to myself. What I understand from this is that if we do what we do, we may never be able to do that. But if we are determined and think we will do it. Then of course we will complete it. This was the first time I was always active day and night, meaning whenever I remembered any new information I was immediately taking notes in that notebook. And at the end of the day I wrote it down. In doing so, I wrote about 150 pages. I mean, I'm surprised to think that 150 pages have come out of my head. Really amazing.

I will not say that you can change the world if you read this book. But what I will say is that if you read this book, you will change yourself a little bit. Even a little change in your thinking will happen. I have written down many of the things I feel in the book. And I'm not an experienced writer. I have never studied literature, so I do not have much knowledge about literature, because I am a science student. And I will make sure that such mistakes do not happen again. This is my first book so I have no experience in that way. My purpose is not to make money by selling books. So you can download and read this book in any way you want. I will be happy if you read. Because my purpose is to read this book if you have a point in your life

I would consider myself very lucky if you can make a difference. That I was able to come to your work. I have no bad intentions behind writing this book. Why I thought maybe you should read a book like this. Maybe by reading this book you will learn to be good. Start giving yourself time.

We always try to change the people around us but if you read the book you might start to change yourself first. Because only if I change myself first can I change the people around me and the world.

I may have completed this book in 14 days, that's right but I have 18 years of experience in writing this book. I have tried to write this book with lessons from what happened to me. I don't know how you feel about the book, but I hope it's good

It takes.

I have tried to talk about the small things in our lives, I don't know exactly how many words I have been able to convey to you. But I tried my best.

We have tried to explain to you little by little on every subject from our studies to love, so that we can find the right purpose in our lives.

Because life is ours, so our purpose is to find out who we are. Otherwise, if we give it to others, they can play with our life. It's a lot like when we give our favorite thing to someone else, they don't like it, they just need it.

We need to understand these things.

In doing so, I finished the book. I would like to write several more books if you have prayers. I will write them down.

You will be fine, take care of yourself.

Mominul Amin

ONE

HOW ARE YOU?

Are you okay ?

Have you had a good day?

With whom you spend every day. Do they care about you?

At the end of the day, they ask you how you spent the day?

Ever been upset at the end of the day?

Ever wanted to die?

Ever wonder if I could do that, maybe to be a little better than you are today? Sleep well at night. Now, don't you get angry with me?

The people of the world think they're acting with you.

Parents don't get angry that they don't want to fulfill their dreams through you, which they couldn't do. And these are their dreams that seem to make sense to you.

I never thought it would change the world.

Never thought that tomorrow would be a better day.

Never want to buy something you want to buy, but you may not be able to afford it.

Are you happy in the end?

You mean, like, saltines and their ilk, eh?

If any of the questions I asked above happen to you or match one,

Then the book is for you or my words are for you.

Do we want too much from society.

Nato?

Just want to be a little happier, want to be a little better.

That's what we get.

I don't have to answer the above questions, ask the questions yourself and answer them yourself.

See the answers you give yourself, whether you give them from the heart, or whether you are satisfied with the answers you give.

I hope not.

There is not a word

Whoever I want, I want someone else

First of all, do I really know or do we really know why we want him?

Isn't it?

We want to do a lot of big things in life. Or we want someone to be a businessman or a great photographer. So maybe we don't have a mind to study at all. So maybe our reading seems to understand what it is not.

So what we have done in life, we have done some of it, I mean better.

I mean, the things we want to do in life, do you think you want to be a photographer?

But have you ever clicked a good type of photo, which is enough to become your photographer?

Didn't, that's why. That means you just want to be a photographer but you don't want to work on that.

Isn't that so.

And one thing I always say is that no one in the world understands us, parents, brothers and sisters and even friends.

Do you understand yourself?

I don't think so.

That's right.

I did not want to confuse you by asking so many questions. My only intention was that you can recognize yourself even if it is a little bit through my words.

Because if we can't recognize ourselves.

Then the people of the world will recognize our ashes.

Not so.

Do you love someone

If yes, then surely he has hurt you sometimes or his words or his actions have hurt you.

Maybe you wanted to explain things to him but you may have been scared.

If I say that I am hurt for all these reasons, then maybe he will quarrel with you.

The biggest, he could leave.

This fear is not so

And if you don't love someone or simply say you're single.

For you to be single in your friends circle, your friends may have questioned your ability to seduce your daughter.

Isn't that so.

Seeing your friend's expensive car expensive phone

What do you want to buy.

You may not be able to afford it because of poor financial condition.

So maybe you are arrogant towards God.

Maybe your friend is more qualified than you to carry an expensive car or an expensive phone, to carry an expensive phone or an expensive car.

That's right

Have you ever thought that your friends might have gone to good college? Or maybe he did well because he got a good school.

You may not have received the benefits.

Your results have not been as high as you expected.

Doesn't it look boring?

Hey no no I'm not boring you.

Only I am raising the questions in your mind for once.

Because it is best to question yourself.

Hey, I forgot.

How can you not ask yourself?

Because you don't have time. After a long day of talking, you may not be able to find time for yourself.

Do not question yourself.

That's why you have to give yourself a little time.

You can wait all day for the girl you love.

But look you couldn't make time for yourself.

Then how will the people of the world spend their time talking to you.

Do you think that the situation you have now will last a lifetime?

I mean if you're good.

Or spend the whole day having fun with friends. And think that in this way the whole life may pass or you may pass.

And if you are bad, do you think that you will be bad this way all your life?

No boss you won't stay.

Remember that everything in the world has the opposite.

And if you are good, be prepared for the dangers ahead.

And if you're bad.

But give good tidings to your heart,

That your good times are about to come.

Believe in God?

If you do well, if you do not, then do not start.

God or not will at least give you peace of mind.

Because even if it is for a while, you will put your problems on God's shoulders.

This is what is needed.

You cannot carry all the burdens of the world alone.

Hey, you are human.

From the burden of all your own suffering, you don't understand that you leave something to someone who thinks he is God.

If you ask me a personal question,

Who are you, God?

But the answer is yes.

But I am a very God fearing person.

Hey I always feel like God is watching me.

Which, of course, made the video an overnight sensation.

What should be done?

As a result, I can't do that.

But God did not forbid me.

But because I fear God

The work was not done by me.

Who is the profit here?

Mine

Only by believing in God.

This did not make me think much of Tantric again.

Don't think at all.

Are you ok ?

TWO

IS IT VERY DIFFICULT TO BE GOOD?

Is it too hard to be good?

I don't think so.

In fact we may not know exactly.

That's exactly how happy we should be or how good we should be.

I became sad for no reason.

Don't assume that when we walk down the street or hang out in a store, we get upset when a stranger comes in and makes a bad name for us.

But in whose words we are feeling bad. No, he knows me. No, I know him.

Then catch up again.

Suppose you went to the field to play in the afternoon.

Maybe you went to play for that purpose,

If you go to the field, the body will be better. A little light air will be taken in the body.

He went to the field and saw some boys playing cricket.

You also started playing cricket with them.

Maybe you got out on the first ball.

Just when you see it, your mind will say,

Nothing will happen by me.

No, the purpose of going to the field was yours!

No, playing cricket is the purpose of your life, so that's what you need to say.

Where did you go on the field to freshen yourself up. But he returned home disappointed.

Do we really need all these thoughts?

What did we read all day today?

What did I do?

What did I eat?

But more than that, we think that

What did any boy in the village do today?

Which boy got the job?

Whose new girlfriend is it?

Who bought the new smartphone?

Who bought the new bike?

Who bought the new house?

We are not a little more interested in these issues.

What is needed at all.

The above is because we do not have the things or what we have may not be of that quality.

We suffer, we feel sorry for ourselves.

You know for whom you are in trouble.

Or those whose words make you feel bad.

They have good luck.

In fact, we can determine the value of our lives if we want to. In the same way, our well-being is entirely in our hands.

I'm telling you a little story.

I like to be a little fancy. I don't know why, I want everything to be perfect. Everything from clothes to accessories. So that day I was going to meet a friend of mine. I and one of my friends whose name is Devjit. Actually I didn't know how to ride a bike so when I go out I take someone with me. So on the way it suddenly starts to rain. So we have to stop at a place before reaching the biblical place. In that place there is a little porch in front of the house at the back. And we entered the verandah with Devjit and another old man on a bicycle. So there was a sack and I sat on that sack. And my friend Devjit was standing in front of me and the old man was riding the same bicycle

Was doing. What happens if it is raining and there is no tea?

So I asked Devjit to bring tea and he went to fetch tea. I was the only one on the porch and the old man. Suddenly my eyes went to the man's pocket and I saw a note of 100 rupees and two ten rupees with it. And just then I noticed the soles of my feet. He looked at his feet and felt very small. I think I am showing so much arrogance. Or who am I showing these to?

A man's daily earnings I use as shoes.

I don't know why it seems that the old man and I were together that day but still it seems that the older man came from two completely different worlds. How many needs I have how many dreams. And the only thing the old man needs is when the rain will stop and he will go home.

I looked into his eyes and face and saw that there was no pain, no sorrow.

For a while, everything I had seemed trivial to him. I don't know why the man looked that day as if he was much richer than us. He is much better than us.

He doesn't want to prove anything to anyone. I want to present him in front of people just like that. In it, people can think whatever they want about him. I looked down and saw that everything was perfect. And nothing about that man was perfect. But he thinks he is the best in himself.

And that day I got the real formula for staying well.

And that's when I got the name of this book. "Is it too hard survive well?"

We don't really need everything we're looking for to have a little smile to stay well.

In fact, there is no end to our needs. There is no end to our needs.

There are so many problems in our lives.

I don't really know how much money we need to survive to be good. Because when we start earning we forget everything and just start earning. Then one day we die.

I'm not saying we don't need money to survive.

Of course there are plenty needed.

But we have to stop for a while.

You must try to move forward but I will never forget what you have.

We struggle to keep the people we love well. A lot of times I struggle to keep my family well.

You know your family can never be good if you are in trouble.

And those who are good to you with suffering are not at least your family members.

So understand things a little bit.

THREE

How Many Friends Do You Need?

Friend friend friend

Our happy partner, our sad partner

Even our partner in bad deeds.

How we live depends a lot on the people around us.

You know that.

I mean, a lot of what we do and how we live is in the hands of our friends.

It's a little surprising, but it's true.

You may be thinking that all this is in our own hands.

Then you are thinking wrong.

Suppose you have four friends. With whom you spend most of your leisure time. There is nothing to say about the purpose of each of them except you. They spend most of the day intoxicated or playing games.

If you tell them something good.

Or say something about the purpose of life, then you will see that they will not pay attention to you.

You will feel once in a while.

Let's play games with them.

That way when you play games with them you will never realize that your game has become addictive.

Or pulling a couple of cigarettes away from them and you yourself become a real addict.

You never understand.

Suppose you have five friends. Each of them has a purpose in life. You have no purpose in life. And the cigarettes in your group just say you eat.

Then you will see that the purpose of your life has come when you listen to the conversations of your friends. In the same way since they do not smoke cigarettes. So you can't smoke while you are with them.

So gradually you too will come out of the intoxication.

Now you understand.

What we become or what we think depends a lot on the people around us.

I'm not judging anyone here.

I'm just trying to explain the reality to you. Neither do I dislike smoking, nor do I smoke cigarettes.

Try to understand the language of what I said.

Now again we are more than real people or chatting with friends in the afternoon.

I give a little more time to my Facebook friends.

Not so.

We always say. How many friends of the car. He uploaded the picture today. How many likes did it get? Who reacted? We like to think more of these. A recent study found that a person can't talk to virtual people as much as 10%.

Or suppose your mother fell ill yesterday. Will your Facebook friends come?

Of course the answer is no.

When you know they won't come. So there is a real benefit to spending so much time behind them.

Of course not?

Again our friend will be angry that he is admitted to this school or college. We also get admitted to make him happy.

Whatever the goal of our life.

We make him our friend from time to time.

We think we are making friends.

After some time, I see those friends who hurt us.

We are often the reason behind being bad.

I'm not forbidding you to make friends, I'm just trying to figure out who you're going to make friends with.

I'm not asking him to match the lineage. All I'm saying is that before you make friends or trust someone, check to see if the person you're going to make friends with is the right person for you.

If the answer is yes, then make sure.

But if not, never make it.

You may be thinking, hey, I'm just making a friend. If you think so much, you can't mix with anyone. That's why I first asked you, do you want to be good?

I want to be happy in life.

And for that you have to accept or start accepting everything little by little.

You are in the category of people who want to be good.

You may think that you have asked for a little. But do you know that the most valuable thing you can do in the world is to stay hollow.

We like to be alone a lot of the time.

As the present age progresses, we are slowly becoming lonely.

If you look closely, you'll see that you don't hang out with friends like you used to, or hang out with friends like you used to, or you don't even go to the cinema and watch movies, which means you can meet people in those places. You may not like all the places you used to go to. He prefers to spend time with the phone at home. Now let me tell you openly. Just as some friends are bad for us just like a good friend is enough for us. I don't think you need to make more than one friend. Enough if you make a good friend in the right way.

Now you may say that it is very difficult to find good friends these days.

Are you a good friend?

That's right.

Can't believe it?

If I make friends with you, are you my bad friend?

What's worse than yourself, as a friend.

No,

So?

You see, we always hear that no friend is good. All you need is just mix.

Then you are thinking wrong.

If you think for yourself, don't think lightly but think very deeply.

You mix that with friends yourself.

Do you just mix with them? If you think very deeply, you will not see Mess.

You will also see that there are some hidden interests. Maybe your interest is smaller than the one in front. But there are interests.

If you do not mix without interest. Then how will the rest do it.

Let me be clear

At first you think just how many very good friends you have. Those who will rush to your word in times of danger. Don't miss out on any friends. But remember only that friend who always comes to you in one word. At the same time remember that he should come to you without any interest.

If you have a name in Uttara then you are a very lucky person. And if the answer is no, then this is for you. Or I am for you. If you haven't had such a good friend yet, I'll tell you why.

Have you ever been in danger of them?

Have you ever listened to them?

Stay by their side when they are in danger?

How are they at the end of the day?

Were you happy now? When your time was good. Have you ever remembered them?

Have you ever made them share your happiness?

Think with a little mind. Answer: Will not come.

Imagine for a second you were transposed into the karmic driven world of Earl.

Of course you did with the mind.

But you couldn't make them the people closest to them.

The first thing is that the relationship is always selfless. That means if you mix with someone selflessly. Then you will see that with whom you mix selflessly. She may not be treating you the way you would. But you think a little more and you will see that this is exactly how someone is unselfishly taking care of you. Even listening to all of you.

A little smile is coming, isn't it?

Yeah Al that sounds pretty crap to me, Looks like BT aint for me either, Looks like BT aint for me either, Looks like BT aint for me either, Looks like BT aint for me either, Looks like BT aint for me either, Looks like BT aint for me either.

Just think of them and think we have no one by our side.

Just like some people don't like you, many people love you unselfishly.

So don't think of those who hurt you, but love those who love you. Once you see, you will find good real friends.

We don't need many friends to be truly good.

A friend is enough

That doesn't mean I'm forbidding you to hang out with other friends. For example, if you go to college, you are talking about college friends, if you work in the office, you are talking about your office colleagues, if you go to play in the afternoon, you are talking about your player friendship.

Associate with them but never get involved with them. Unless one of them is your true car friend.

Interact with them first.

Give me some time.

Who made him close to him at times. They will hurt you too.

First of all, do the same thing with a friend before you use it. You don't have to do anything else, he will give you just as much as you deserve.

Yes, but it will take some time.

I mean, you made friends with a stranger. And the behavior you show him is your best behavior. Then at first you may hope that he will also show you very good behavior.

Then you are completely wrong.

He will start to ignore you when he is a few days old after you are gone. Let him ignore.

Because you know you have done everything selflessly with him. Then you can rest assured. He will remember you when someone similarly ignores him and leaves.

This is real.

Tell us about our main problem is the things that we have or the people that we have. When they are with us we see their bad qualities but just when they leave me.

Surprisingly, it is true that we need to remember their good qualities.

And their bad qualities seem insignificant to us then.

We are such a nation.

Got it?

Once you see someone as a good friend, you will be surprised to see that you will never lack a good friend.

By now you must have realized just how much we need friends. I'm talking about good friends here. By now you must have understood exactly how you should be used. Now I will tell you who you want to live as friends. How to find them or know that they deserve to be your true car friend.

I told you first to pick a good friend first. You start it. First we will make good friends from those who are already in your life. Let me help you to make good friends.

The first thing you will notice when choosing a friend is to be a good person in your life. Just how much he respects you and the rest of the people.

What he will notice most is how much he respects poor people. Or how to deal with them. You need JavaScript enabled to view it. Maybe he respects you but doesn't respect anyone else. Then remember that the respect he gives you is not real at all. Maybe there's a big reason he's honoring you today. He is giving you that honor to get something from you. So you can be sure that from the day you don't give him that thing, he will stop respecting you. So if you have such friends already in your life, move away from them as soon as you can. And who speaks with great respect to everyone who is with him, not just you. Interacts with relatives. Then make him a good friend in your life. And you can be sure that he will always be by your side if you are in danger or if your condition ever deteriorates. And if you don't have that kind of person in your life, you keep looking for that kind of person. If you get it, make friends and you will be happy.

Second, the quality of what you do or what you look for in your friend is that the friend doesn't care about the people around him or her.

They love to be very normal. He is happy just as God made him. Then you will remember that no matter who you are, he will always be by your side.

Thirdly, the thing that you will notice the most is exactly how much money it costs you to travel. I mean, if you ever go out with him, he'll tell you to buy it, so buy it. So whenever you go out with them, you have to spend a huge amount. So always stay away from those friends. Because they have come to destroy you.

Aim in the same way if a friend forbids you to spend. Or if he goes to the restaurant a lot of times and pays the bill, then remember that you are very lucky. That's got a good friend. Make him.

Fourth, see if the person you have made or want to be a friend of is lying.

If the answer is yes.

Then move away slowly. The question may come to your mind that nowadays everyone is lying. No, I didn't tell that kind of lie.

Who lies to other friends in front of you who lie about important things. Remember he will lie about you in front of other friends.

So stay away from those who are such friends.

Fifth is one of the most important things you will see among your friends.

Exactly how much they value you. This means that there are many friends who need you or if they need any work. Then he tells you a lot of sweet things, as if there is no better person in his life than you.

But when you need them, they don't pick up your phone properly. It even spends months after months without calling you.

Then you can be sure that you will never find them in danger.

They just mingle with you when they need to. Nothing more than that. So these are very scary. They can tell you everything when they need you. You can do a lot. So always try to stay away from them.

They are the real selfish

They never loved anyone but themselves.

So if you have such friends, remove them from your friends list now.

The sixth thing is to see that everyone in our life has a goal. Meaning there is a purpose to life that you want to do in life. Or you want to work on some things when you grow up. Whenever you say those things in front of your friends, they just make you laugh, or say that these things will not be done by you. Why are you doing these things?

Do the things that we are doing. Lots of money for our work. Keep in mind that those who do not respect your way of thinking can never be your friends. Or can't be your happy partner. So your valuable comments on the way to life with them will not be of any use.

I don't want her to listen to you.

So never tell such friends about your dreams.

The seventh thing to focus on is to stay away from friends who are crazy to get attention from people. Suppose you are in a circle of friends. There is a friend discussing a subject and everyone is listening. Suddenly your friend came and started talking differently. That every friend in that circle of friends began to feel annoyed. And you expect them to listen to you. They are so crazy to get attention from people that your name is in front of you and the other's name in front of others. Just remember that in front of you the other's notoriety confirms your notoriety in front of the other. Because they all want to be good at it all the time. And this is why everyone talks about everything.

So never share with them the important things or secrets of your life. He will always share your secrets with everyone, so if you want to live, stay away from all these friends today.

The eighth thing that is very interesting to see is how he interacts with his family members. You must notice that. I mean, he doesn't listen to his family. Notice if his parents oppose it. Remember that he cannot be his own family, how can he be yours. So you must pay attention to this thing.

You will see that he values his family more or less than you. If you see that one of his family members may have given him something but he is not holding the phone because he is with you, then Moto should not think that he is giving more importance to you. Rather think about it, he doesn't care about his family. She only cares about what she needs so she will always try to stay away from such friends.

How is he to the people of the ninth society. If you see that everyone speaks against him. So you must remember that there must be some flaws in it. If that person is very close to you, find out his faults and let him know.

If he obeys you and corrects that mistake then you are very lucky but if he doesn't then think he is just thinking about himself. So hanging out with him means hurting yourself in the eyes of society. So you are unknowingly making yourself unemployed to the society. The less enemies you make to keep yourself better, the better. So try to stay away from such friends.

The last thing you need to keep in mind is who you are with or who you think is a good friend. What does your mind say is your best friend to win?

Because you can never be happy with good friends if you don't feel good. Can't be better to say more. So keep yourself away from them.

I did not want to belittle anyone with the words I said above. I just tried to explain exactly how you would do to keep yourself well. Exactly how you choose your life friends. Because it's up to you how you live, good or bad.

If you want to keep yourself a little happy, you must choose a good and honest friend.

FOUR

WHAT ELSE TO DO IN LIFE?

"Dreams are not what we see in our sleep
Dreams are what keep us awake. "

If you remember that line, who would tell you that? Our country's President APJ Abdul Kalam.

There are very few people like us who have not heard the quote. But there are few people who know the real meaning of the quote.

In fact we all love to dream. Whether it is asleep or awake.

The dreams we see are beyond our control.

I'm not forbidding to see dreams outside of power but we think that the dreams we are seeing are just that maybe I am seeing. No one else sees.

So I am different than everyone else, I am special.

I dream that I have a purpose in life. I think a lot more than others.

If you think these things then you are thinking completely wrong. If you don't believe, go to that shop and have tea. Ask him out well if he is no longer absorbed in the connection. Want to know about his dreams or friends around you want to know about their dreams. You will see that they have bigger dreams than you. So dreaming is not a big deal. You know why I said this, in fact we all dream.

Dreaming is not a big deal. Exactly how hard we are working to make the dream come true. Not just how hard we are working in the right way will indicate whether my dreams will succeed or not.

You may be wondering what the dream has to do with being good.

Of course there is.

If we want to be good, we have to put a lot of emphasis on everything. The most important thing is to focus on our thoughts and our dreams.

We dream but we do not know what to do to make the dream come true. Again many know but waiting to get started.

If you can't believe it, I'm telling you a story.

I have several YouTube channels like (The MOMI, The smart guide, cinematic Expose, MOMI extra etc) whenever someone watches a video on my channel, especially my friends. They told everyone that they would open their own YouTube channel. They ask me how to open and what to do. I told them to do this. Many of them told me that they were willing to work with me. So what I do is give everyone some elements of making a video and tell them to make a video. Don't believe that maybe every one of them has asked me to do it one day. So, as promised, I call everyone after one day and ask if the work is done. I mean, the video was made. Surprisingly, not everyone told me. Some of them said I didn't really like doing the job. Give if you have other work. And some people said, "Hey, I only have one phone, that's why I couldn't make the video." And some people said give me some more time to make it. The people I gave time to couldn't make a video till today. Every time I call, they tell me to give them some more time.

Surprisingly, one of them made the video. He did not have any expensive phone. No, the boy was more educated. Nor did he have multiple phones. But he made the video in the amount of time he took me. This is what I meant by the small incident above. We don't really want to work. If you really want to do it, don't just sit back and make excuses. But if you look outside, you will see that you want to do what you want to do. The excuse that you are not doing it is just that the other person is doing it even though he has a bigger excuse. Honestly, if we want to do something, nothing can ever stop us. One reason is enough to do something. Enough of an excuse not to do anything in exactly the same way. Whoever wants to do it will do it in spite of thousands of obstacles.

And no matter what you give to those who really don't want to do it, they will find some excuses not to do it.

So if you want to do something in life, start doing it now.

If you think you can't do it, you're wrong. If you can't do something, remember that you can never do anything. Whatever you are doing, whatever you are doing, do it with your mind. You will see that your success is assured.

Do you know one of our biggest faults?

We just don't like what we do. We like other things better and when we do other things we don't like those things but we like the work we used to do.

For example, when we go to school, we make mistakes in everything in the school. For example, the teachers in the school are not good, they don't know how to teach, the school never has any program properly. Again, yes, the school next to us is better. Rahul's school teachers are better. But sadly when we are admitted to Rahul's school we talk about the bad things about that school and say hey there is nothing in the school. Everything was more convenient at the school I attended before.

Now you understand that our problem is in this place.

We ourselves do not know what we want. And that's why we're not good.

I will say one more thing and you will see that one thing is very popular nowadays. Especially when we hear through movies or social media that if you find your passion or find the talent in yourself then your life will become much easier.

And then we fall into confusion. We keep wondering what talent we have. And what we see is that we have no talent. We can sing properly. No we are too beautiful to look at. No, our parents have a lot of money, we will do whatever we want. Then we see a lot of frustration. That's when we remember that friend of mine sings well, that friend is very beautiful to look at and so on.

Which leads us to depression. For some reason we continue to blaspheme God. If God did not give us anything, then why did He send us to earth only to be insulted by the people?

You see how bad our thinking is.

First of all, there is no such thing as talent. And if anyone thinks that there is something called talent, then remember that there must be some talent in each of us. God did not just make us. There must be some purpose behind its making. He created everything in the world for a purpose. He never created anything without purpose.

Now why are you thinking these things for those who do not obey God?

Everybody thinks that we have sent a white paper by God with some talent in some people which means we have written something on his white paper. And if you think that I have no talent, then you think that you did not write anything on your white paper. Then you see how much advantage you have, you can write whatever you want on that white page as you wish, you can even write as much as you want. And whoever has something written on his page already has no right to do more in life. He has some limited intelligence. But you have many options to prove yourself the best in the world.

Now you tell me who is really lucky?

Believe me you don't have to worry about it. Think about it again what you have. Honestly, if you keep counting, you will see that you are happier than I am. You will find that you have so many things that you may have never thought of before. The biggest thing is that the things you have may not be very good people. The thing you've been thinking about for so long must be gone.

Now let's see what we have to do. To say that we will do any work in life as a livelihood. Or which way to go. I think the first thing you need to do before asking this question is. You just have to be more discriminating with the help you render toward other people.

Because every decision we make depends on our past thinking. To put it better, it depends on past experience.

We can never be good if we do not choose the right path to earn a living.

So in order to be good, we have to look at all these things very well.

I mean you see I have a problem that we always have more vacation behind to make the next dream a success.

If you can't believe it, I'm explaining.

Suppose the boy next to me has taken science. As a result, the people around her date her all the time. But I want to do Honors in English with the Arts. Because I like to read English. But maybe you don't believe me and I will start studying science. I say why because people say they will appreciate me. Or that he has taken science means that the certainty is better.

This is where we sit by mistake. That's why we are never good. And we unknowingly follow the next dream.

Now you understand how we always follow the next dream.

I studied on missions from a young age so I noticed one thing. Nana didn't notice it at a young age. That's what I thought about when I was growing up.

When some of my friends were in fifth grade, their dreams were medical engineer, barrister, astronaut and so on.

Then when they were in class XI and XII, their dreams were so strong.

What would you do in life? Someone said I would be the richest man in the world.

Who said I would be the most famous astronaut in the world?

Someone said I would be a cricketer?

I would tell them it was no longer possible. If anyone in the world had done that, they would have told me the example of that person.

"Why can't I have that person on earth?"

I was quite surprised by their confidence.

But when I asked those friends in college life, what will you do in life?

It's very sad to hear, but it's true

That they told me it would be a normal job.

You must be able to relate.

This is how our dreams slowly begin to end with life.

And we begin to blame God or the situation.

Isn't that so?

Honestly, it is not God's fault or our situation that is behind our dreams.

If anyone is really to blame, it is our own fault.

Because we have the right dream at a young age and when it is time for us to make this dream a success. When we are old enough to work.

Or studying in college. Then we just waste time chatting and hanging out with friends. As a result, we do not understand how beautifully we ruin our lives.

Blame it on the situation.

I mean, it's not too late now.

Start today or start now.

Whatever you want to do.

Do it in such a beautiful way. And do it with such a mind that no one else can do that job better than you.

This means that if you work as a cobbler along the railway line, you do it so well and with so much love that no one else in the area can do cobbler work well.

Believe that you will earn twice as much money as you need to survive.

We never really do anything with the mind. When I do that, I don't give importance to that work as my next job.

So if someone ever asks you what are you doing in life?

Then you never have to say it.

I don't do anything like that anymore.

Say yes instead I'm doing it.

And say that with pride.

Never underestimate what you do. Imagine for a second you were transposed into the karmic driven world of Earl.

So how do you expect the rest of the people to respect your work?

The jobs I talked about here are applicable to all cases if you are a student or if you work in an office.

Without looking hard at the events happening around you. Try simply watching.

You will see that everything looks clear.

Try to understand yourself the most. Give yourself time.

Talk to yourself.

Keep trying to solve every problem with a cool head.

One of our biggest problems was that we always wanted to do everything together.

Have you ever wondered if it is possible to go from Kolkata to Delhi together?

So do what you need to do first or what is most important in your life. Do it well then do the rest of the work.

For example, I will go where I need to go first and then I will go next.

I hope things are clear to you.

FIVE

WANT TO LOVE SOMEONE?

Love is something that every human being in the world is involved with. Which is something all over the world that cannot be imagined or imagined.

There are so many fairy tales about love, so many stories have been written that it would seem trivial for people like me to write there.

The most important thing behind our well-being is love. Be it parents, be it brothers and sisters, be it friends. So if we understand this thing exactly. Then I think we will get the solution to our problem.

Yeah Al that sounds pretty crap to me, Looks like BT aint for me either.

But if I can explain to you what I have understood with my knowledge, then you will find the real purpose of love, even if only a little.

We find very few people who have not fallen in love unknowingly. If we cry the most in life we cry for love and if we get the most joy in life we get it for love.

In the present age, thousands of students are ruining their lives in the wrong way for not understanding love properly. We are among them.

I am starting from a very young age and with simple language.

God said that I sent love to earth to experience what Paradise or Heaven would be like, which is only one percent of the happiness of Paradise.

So tell me, if God sends love to experience what paradise or heaven can be, how can we suffer from it?

It will give us so much joy that we will realize that if we do good deeds on earth, we will go to heaven or paradise. And how much happiness there will be.

But the way love is hurting us in today's society, I don't think anyone will ever want to go to paradise.

So I don't think God ever told a lie, of course we have a misunderstanding.

Isn't that so?

Of course it is.

We start with the biggest mistake. Every time we see a beautiful girl on the street, at an event, at school or college, we fall in love with her. I have been busy impressing him ever since. If I can impress him, then so be it. For the first few days in the world, it feels like I am in a dream world. Then slowly when I see each other's real form, then one of the two suffers and the other suffers.

Isn't that so?

The first thing we need to know is what is love?

Why do we love?

You see, we have a tendency. If someone asks us why we love, we answer that. We need someone who will understand us and love us as we are. We will share each other's words and share each other's troubles. You are right.

This time I say I think love is happening

"It's just a name to enjoy each other's bodies"

If it didn't exist then why love. You could have built a friendship with him in general. He could have made her a better sister. Couldn't even share about these two that I could after love I would say I couldn't just share the physical needs I could do everything else.

When our purpose is not right. Then how can we be happy or be good for that wrong purpose.

I am not opposing love here. I am just trying to explain the real meaning of love. If we truly love someone then why should we touch him. Don't be impatient for him. If not after marriage, he touched her. And if you can't bear that much, how can you share the suffering of that man in times of danger?

Then there will be patience.

I'm telling you in very simple language that is why we love?

There comes a time in our lives when we leave childhood and become adults. It is only then that we slowly begin to realize that we are beginning to be separated from our family members. That's when we find someone to tell our failure stories or to make ourselves feel a little special and that's the man we love.

You can love someone with good intentions. I don't think there is ever anything wrong with that. But in exactly the same way if you do not touch him. However, you can swear not to hurt.

But what do we do? We made each other's parents villains. And I think the world does not understand our love. How will the world understand? Your love You do not understand what your love is.

I'm talking about a boy and a girl. That you have not understood the love of your family for so long. In your few minutes of love, you can forget the love of your family for so long. So how can you be sure. That he will never forget your love.

Now open your head.

Love can never hurt anyone. If that is the right way. But you see, in the present love, we continue to hurt our parents, family and society.

If your love is so sacred. And if your parents understand that. Then why don't you get married?

Because you want to be just as good. Your parents want to keep you better than that.

Surely they think your love is not right. Because they have seen the world more than you have. That doesn't mean they know everything. I mean, explain to them why you should be good to them.

The movies of our present age, who love is in such a way, show you that your parents are villains and you are heroes.

No, the parents are villains. No, you are heroes. Something is wrong with you, something is wrong with your parents.

Try to understand each other's situation and then you will be able to find a good and correct solution. Not before that.

We buy clothes from a good shop. I bought food and chess from a good shop. But when we pick the most valuable people in our lives, we see nothing. A quality we like temporarily. Well, that's a good reason for us to love someone.

And you think that person will keep you well. Or you'll be better off by it. Of course you will have multiple troubles with him. He may leave you in the future. My point is that you are the most precious thing in your life. You give the most valuable place in your life to someone.

Now at least think a little.

Where I am telling you to check so much in choosing a friend I will not say here anymore.

What do you really think.

I tell you love. Love too much, love too much.

Yes, love the girl.

But you know if you love properly.

Then never throw mud on each other during breakup like the lovers of the present society.

Build relationships that I mean. So that the man you love on the first day, just as much as you like him, more than just him, when you leave him or he will leave you. Then there is a lot of respect for each other. This time you may be thinking that maybe I am telling you a fairy tale.

No nono

If you start to love a girl right. No, then your relationship will be better than a fairy tale.

Imagine for a second you were transposed into the karmic driven world of Earl. Then how beautiful will be the stories of God made about us.

You might think badly, in fact we don't know how to love?

Okay I can answer the question. But give the answer with your hand on your chest.

There are three things you can do with the person you love. The first is holiness. I'm talking about holiness, not just physical relationships but mental relationships.

I mean, never touch or touch each other before marriage, no matter what.

Secondly, respect for each other. No matter how bad the situation has been, there has never been a time when they have never lost respect for each other.

Third, trust in each other. No matter how bad people call each other by name. You didn't believe this had happened.

And if you accept these three things, you will never know where your relationship will go.

Now you understand why I am saying what is wrong with your love. Now there are many of you, hey, we will marry each other. Then what happens when you have a physical relationship.

Imagine for a second you were transposed into the karmic driven world of Earl.

Then!

You both cheated on those who later married you.

Isn't that so.

And you are talking about love.

Hey, if we love someone these days, we keep asking for his picture on WhatsApp on the second day. If not, we threaten to leave.

We are going through this dirty kind of relationship. And you think this relationship will make you happy. No bad thing is good for too long.

Remember one thing is worse than worse. But if you had a sacred relationship with someone

There was no reason to leave each other.

Your family has no reason to refuse.

And even then, if he had left, you would have loved the wrong person. Or God has kept your worthy daughter for you.

Now you will say that these words are very good as proverbs.

Then you are thinking completely wrong. We don't get a lot of things a lot of the time. Then we feel bad and we hate God. To take that thing away from us for not giving it. Later, when God gives us something better than that, we realize the reason for taking that thing away from us. We can never be wiser than God. A lot of times when you want nude pictures of your loved ones. And if he doesn't give it to you then maybe you will feel very bad.

You will feel that you could not believe this little bit.

You think once you do not love her body?

Of course that's right

Will love to touch people too much. You must be patient for that. This time you may say I can't bear it.

That doesn't mean it's a lot like that. You started insisting that I should be a big police officer today. Is that possible? No, that's only possible if you work hard and be patient enough to be a police officer and wait for the right time.

Then it's time for you to be patient and wait.

So why can't you be patient for the most precious thing in your life?

Things are very small but very deep.

When we are in a relationship with each other. Then we have to try to take care of each other enough.

I mean, if I say more clearly, I mean that.

When your opposite partner wants to have a physical relationship with you or something about that will appeal to you.

Then you will interrupt him mentally without interrupting him directly. And if you don't tell him at that time, he will misunderstand you a little more, instead of understanding you.

So if you see something wrong with your partner, try to resolve it from his side without leaving him.

And if you think that I will find a perfect man. Believe me you will never get it.

We will find someone perfect, better than that we will make someone perfect.

Maybe it will take a while. But the fruit you get will give you a little more joy.

SIX

WHAT PEOPLE WILL SAY?

The biggest is "What People Will Say"

What people will say is no less than a panic to us.

If you do not get a job, it is as much a problem as the people in your household. People in the neighborhood think more than that.

Hey, if you start doing something, why can't you do it from all around. People will come to you for that reason. So it is one of the biggest problems in our lives.

Isn't that so?

Catch your daughter, who ran away with a boy. A few months later when you found out they were fine. And what could be better news for you than having your daughter well. You will then think of calling them home. And that's exactly what people will say in your head. Then you can't bring the girl home anymore.

Suppose again that you dropped out of a class. And after failing, you realized your mistakes and you decided to re-enter the class for the second time. And this time I will correct the mistakes and get good results. It will tell your mind but when you think a little in your head you will start to think what people will say if I read for the second time in the same class.

If you want to color your hair to fulfill your hobby, you can't, you will think if people say something.

Now you realize how big a problem it is. You can never be good if you can't overcome it.

We need to understand what we need and what we don't need. Do what you need to do now.

One thing to keep in mind is that you should not do anything that hurts or hurts a person. You can do whatever you want without hurting or hurting anyone. Even if thousands of people say that.

People used to say when you were little. And still people say and will continue to say in the future. So never sing about them. Because every time you listen to them, you hurt yourself. Or asking yourself to hurt them.

Remember that you have got life once so don't let it get lost.

You come to earth, stay for a while, then leave.

You don't want to do anything for yourself, for your family, for this world. Then God's creation is in vain.

I think God sends every human being on earth with some or the other quality. And if you don't put that quality in front of the world. So God gave us a gift Habra missed or we lost, isn't it?

Talking to people You know when people talk about you when he tried to do what you are doing but he couldn't do it so he forbade you that you can't either.

Here he is not forbidding you but trying to convince you how much you deserve more than him.

Never take what people are saying badly.

Remember that their words will help you reach your goal. They are inspiring you Maybe their way of saying is bad but their motive is not bad.

And if you are afraid of people's words. Then not only the work that you are doing but also the work that you cannot do in front of you for fear of people.

Like people are telling you, why don't you get a job?

You took their words very seriously and got a government job. You think they will appreciate you, not at all. You know what they say!

"It's not your job, the salary is low. My nephew's son is your age. He earns twice as much as you."

So never listen to them and impress them. Because they will never be happy with any of your work.

So leave them to impress. Rather impress those who care about you and love you. If something happens to you, they will suffer.

Listen to them.

You will see that you have many such friends in your life. Those who try to make themselves better make you sad.

Suppose you did something. Here I try to illustrate with examples.

Suppose you bought a car. Then your friend will come to you and say that the car is good but, Rahul was saying that the color of the car is not good. I told him that this color is the best. Here they were the real purpose he wanted to be good to you. But he did not realize that he had hurt you. These kinds of people are the most horrible. Try to stay as far away as you can from surviving. These are the people for whom you say that you have done nothing for them even after doing everything. Now you understand which of my friends I am

I'm talking.

I'm talking about the friends you think.

In fact, there is a saying that outsiders can never hurt us. Always give the people who are closest to us.

And that is what we understand.

People are not actually outsiders. People are always our relatives and friends.

In fact, who are you? It creates a fear in your mind. Never think of them as part of your life.

Every day 60 to 70 thousand bad thoughts come into our heads. And the one thing that bothers us the most is "what people will say."

And the more we think about it, the more we will hand over the remote control to others.

The more we think about it, the more we start listening to people. We all know these words but why do these words stay in our heads?

The answer is very simple?

Because they try to hit him with our all time weak focal point. Which makes us everything

Despite knowing, people are forced to listen. Then why do we listen to them?

If I try to explain it a little bit, I will see that we are always dependent.

This is why I am trying to explain a little more why I am saying this.

Suppose you go to tuition every day. So one day you thought that you will not go to tuition today, instead you will go to see a movie. On the way to the cinema, you meet a person whom you call Kaka. Has seen you Here you will be afraid that if he tells you at home, he will scold you. Here you are not afraid of that old man. You are afraid of your parents. This is exactly what we people are not afraid of. I am afraid that those people will stand up so that none of our own people will suffer.

If I bully on the street. Then maybe what people will say. That's what I think. The idea is that when people tell me about my own people, they will suffer for my behavior.

If we try to explain it more accurately, it will be a lot like,

Suppose you have failed at something in your life. You will see that you will be afraid to do that job for the second time. If you fail this time, what will people say about you? It is a fear shown to us. But the real fear is inside. That when we failed for the first time, the people who were with us were also hurt by our family members and they were harmed by me. And I don't want to hurt and hurt them in the same way by failing a second time. So I am afraid of the words of my people.

And that's what we need to do to get out of here. That we have to think like that without thinking like that. That is the second time we want to do this so that the people who live with us can live with their heads held high.

So when we find the right purpose for something. We don't think about people anymore.

On the way to life, always try to keep the purpose behind doing something right. You will see that no one else cares about you. Brother, if we can do it. We will be able to solve this big problem.

SEVEN

I DON'T CARE

I don't care"

I was anno

Anyon yed to hear that. Hey you will see the content of television starting from social media. I don't care about anyone.

The students of class five write in their bio. I don't care what the world is saying. And now there is one more thing. Now we show the middle finger to show that I don't care about anyone. To show yourself cool in the eyes of society.

When I was in class twelve. Then I saw that on the day when Mother's Day was read, everyone would write Happy Mother's Day with status. With a picture of his mother.

But I could not pay. That's why I'm a little shy. I also thought I love my mother so much so why not give it to me. I used to see everyone give status when someone from their own family dies. But I could not pay. I felt very guilty then. But slowly as I learned to understand I saw that when we care about something or when someone cares about us we really don't understand the importance of them. Someone left and we realized the status. I never gave status because my love never diminished. When your man dies. Then you can't put his status.

That's why we don't care.

I don't say I don't care, I say I care. Because if you don't really care about something, you don't think about it. Then why don't you go write that I don't care.

First of all we take care of everything. When we don't like a person, we don't tell everyone that I don't like him, but I don't go to the places where he is talked about.

Not so.

Secondly, why do you think that caring is bad?

Must understand, must know.

I don't understand how much I have hurt others to make myself look cool in front of everyone.

We must care We must care. If we care for someone, he will care for us.

Imagine for a second you were transposed into the karmic driven world of Earl. Will it ever be okay to show that.

Why show the middle finger?

When you grow up. Then you know when you open your Facebook, you will see. That is, you have uploaded a picture showing the middle finger. You will laugh at yourself that day and think how stupid you were.

Have your children look at the pictures you want and think about how their parents were.

One thing to keep in mind is that our future depends on what we are doing now. If we don't make a mistake now, we will have to pay for it in the future.

If we say we have a problem, we always expect good behavior from the people in front of us. But we ourselves do not treat anyone well. This time you may say

You are wrong Yes, when we say we behave well, when we have interests. In fact, the people of the world are not selfish, we are selfish ourselves. We will say we don't care about anyone and people will take care of us.

It would be a mistake to use the word 'I don't really care'. This time he said why do we actually care.

If you think a little better you will see that when we were children but we didn't really care for anyone.

Suppose you are forced into the lap of an IPS officer as a child. And if you get your urine at that time, you will do it immediately.

You don't think for once that you are in someone's lap.

That's right.

But if you are asked to stand in front of an IPS officer, you will be scared to stand.

That's right!

Please tell, whats the story of them big puppys ..... It is caused by fear. Because if you see you didn't listen to anyone when you were younger. Besides, you didn't care about anyone. But gradually as you get older, everyone in your society, from your relatives to you. Began to ban on small things.

Like don't do this, don't do that, doing this will hurt you. Doing so will make you sick. We get used to hearing such things from a young age. Which is when we come of age.

Then that child is no longer with us. We get rejection from people so many times in life. Which is why we are afraid to think of small things. I can do it.

This society kills the brave being in us. As a result, we grow up, but we are scared.

As a result, we are afraid to do whatever we want. To put it bluntly, we first see the bad side of starting a business. And that's where I stopped that work. It is our biggest disease.

If you look, you will see that I said at the beginning of the book that people are afraid to dream as they grow up. You mean, like, saltines and their ilk, eh? You will see that he will say medical engineer astronaut

Etc. But if you ask him after 22 years what you want to be. Then the boy will say that even a small job will work. It is a fear of our failures. Slowly our good being seems to be losing the courageous truth somewhere.

Have you ever thought about this before?

Hopefully not.

There is no question of not caring for anyone here.

We have to go inside the problems and understand who, we have to know. Otherwise we will never be able to find the solutions to the problems above.

I mean, we have to wake up the dead, or the brave, in our minds. Until we can wake it up. Until then we can't be good. No matter how old we get, we should never kill the child in us.

Now we are talking about how that brave child among us died?

You may think the answer is difficult, but not at all.

In fact, we have killed this entity through our multiple minor mistakes.

Suppose we never study with the mind. As a result, we did not do well in class. Then you will be afraid to read us. Every time we are afraid of something. Only then will the brave being in us slowly die.

But the society did not kill the brave truth here. I died because of your own mistakes.

That's right.

I've been saying from the beginning of the book that we have to look at everything very well in order to be good. We need to know what we need.

None more.

How to tell now is also very straightforward. Correct your mistakes that can still be corrected. And keep it in your head so that you don't make unnecessary mistakes in front of you. In fact, if you always lead yourself in the simple, straight and true path, that brave truth will never die in you.

The more the maya of the world grows in our minds, the more the wrong deeds and the wrong path will continue through us. As long as these continue, the brave child in us will continue to die.

As a result, we will continue to fail in whatever we do. Every time we fail, frustration, sadness, jealousy, anger, etc. Will come down in us.

It's really hard to say anything and turn it into reality. We need to understand exactly what we are saying. Because we are creating a wrong image in the eyes of the people in the society through our wrong message which is not needed at all.

This time you may have a question in your mind again. You said a little while ago that society does not have to accept. Now you are saying that the society has to accept. First of all, I never said that society does not have to accept. Because whether you like it or not, we complement each other. So you can never develop without society and society without you. Simply put, it will never work without each other. Once you think about what you are saying, you will remain in that society and I will not call you a member of the society. Or you will neglect the society in which you live.

Society can never be bad. You have to remember that there are two sides to every thing, one is bad and the other is good. And this is no exception.

My purpose can never be to tell you to be alone. Because you don't feel good when you're alone.

By this time, I hope you have understood that we should not say who cares and who should not. If you ask me I would say no one should tell. Why would you say something to someone you don't like?

EIGHT

MY PARENTS DON'T UNDERSTAND ME

If there is anyone closest to us in the world, it is these two parents. But whenever we are a little bigger. Not mentally towards the body when we grow up. Then we don't like our parents. In the modern age, we are constantly proving our parents wrong in order to present ourselves as smart in front of everyone. We forget that we start talking to them holding their hands.

At present we all have a complaint. You see, I want to do it, my dad won't let me do it. Or I want to buy it, Mom doesn't buy it.

Nowadays we have so much influence ourselves on social media. We think that the direction they have given us is the right one. That means they will see a word and follow your passion. And from then on we started to follow. Then we start to indulge

I have to be a singer so I will drop out of school.

I want to paint.

I want to act.

I started talking like this to my parents. And then they scold us and when we hear that we think that they are not by our side. In fact, they do not understand me. From then on we start doing whatever we like. Out of pride we begin to stop talking to our parents. Not talking to parents. As a result, we never understand when we have slowly moved away from them. Without them we have begun to organize our lives. I started walking alone. Now tell me who is to blame here, not us or our parents. Nor did they ever tell us to separate from them. To put it more bluntly, have you ever explained to them what you want to be? Then how will they understand what you want to be. If you can't figure out what talent you have, how can they find it in you?

Just think, you have a son. He came to you and said, "Dad, I will not study." I will be a cricketer. How do you feel?

No he has played a big match before. Maybe he didn't play with anyone except the boys in the neighborhood. He doesn't even play better than all the boys in the neighborhood. He may have hit sixes in just a few days and the villagers have encouraged him so he wants you to be a cricketer.

This time he said that you will accept him by giving up his studies.

Never.

One thing to keep in mind is that the decisions we make are not always connected to the past. Maybe your parents wanted to do something in life but they couldn't. Due to various difficulties, so maybe in your decision, they can see their past money.

A past where there is only destruction.

Then think about it, they don't want you to be ruined like them. So don't get angry with them. Explain things to them. Let them see what you want to do. You are doing it right. You will see that your parents will buy the things you need to do the job, no matter how expensive.

Once you understand them, you will get all the answers.

You know there are some things in life that we don't realize until we get to that place. That's exactly where the parents' place is.

No matter what I mean to you. Why don't you read thousands of novels. You won't understand them properly unless you are someone's father. When you are, you will see that everything will be clear to you. You will have clear answers to the questions you want to ask your parents today.

But then you will repeatedly go back in time and feel guilty for doing bad things to them.

It will hurt yourself not to spend time with them.

You will see them hugging each other and wanting to cry. But you may see that they may not be in this world.

And then you will continue to look for your father among older people. Talk to them now without finding your father in the future. You smile openly with them. You may not know how much you value them. You know that no matter how much they suffer, if you talk to them once in front of them with a smile, all their sorrows will go away.

Now one thing you will notice is that we now go from village to town to study or stay for work. There we do not want to introduce ourselves to the parents in our village to always prove ourselves the best.

I wonder what my friends will say if my parents don't wear such clothes.

What if my girlfriend thinks I'm poor and leaves?

One thing to keep in mind is that those who really love you don't care how you are. Where did you come from? So every person who is with you is involved in your life. So never separate them. It is a matter of pride for you to have your parents no matter who they are. So never hide them.

They make you proud.

NINE
FAKE WORLD

Fake fake fake ......

Fake is a very familiar and used word today. Everywhere you look today, the things you buy, the things you eat, the things you read are all involved in this fake word.

Things seem to be fake as people slowly don't know why. Doesn't even their use seem fake?

This word is like a poison to us today. Scattered all around. It needs to stop now.

Because this is what is stopping us from being the best. So we have to find out. That is where this word is being used in our lives.

We have to stop those things. We will not be good until we can stop it.

Now I am trying to analyze the issues slowly.

Nowadays we like to show people. If you can't believe it, you will see any people's social media like WhatsApp, Facebook, Instagram. And go there and see their lifestyle. It would seem that one Dhoni is better than the other. It seems that there is no problem in their life. And if you look at them in real life, you will see that one is in more trouble than the other. One is poorer than the other. By seeing them we are busy proving that we are greater than them and that we are greater than them.

No matter how many problems there are in our lives.

We gradually forgot what we needed. Anything we need. We just took it now so I have to take it.

And how long we will continue to fulfill the next dreams.

If he doesn't need it, then why should I take it?

I started with a short story, I was then studying in a hostel in Burdwan. Everyone there smoked cigarettes. So one day I was sitting next to a boy eating and I asked him brother why are you smoking?

Eating like this to show yourself modern.

Hey, you eat too, it's a trend these days. Hey everyone, if you don't play it, men again. Moreover, it can not be enjoyed without playing.

If you want to be modern, do you really have to smoke cigarettes?

Not really.

You smoke to make yourself look better than others.

You don't need it and you don't need it to be a model.

Now I am studying in college so it seems like I will understand when I will grow up in a few days and when I will not be able to leave it. It was never a trend.

And then I'll see if you can't leave it. It's too late.

As a result, I've never smoked a cigarette, because for some reason I didn't feel good about myself.

That means I'm not underestimating those who eat.

This is exactly the style of governing the country that he has used in Russia.

We all think of ourselves as celebrities these days. Trying to show people like them in front of people. And the beginning is right here. The boy bought a good camera. I also need it. You may not understand. Not that we were ever celebrities. Now we are young so we have time to show ourselves as celebrities. When not to get. You know how bad you feel when you face reality. Who were you showing? And the biggest thing is that you have given up enjoying your life by exposing this false life in front of everyone.

First of all, where is your life? But you know why you don't get happiness. Because you are trying to follow the life of others instead of enjoying your own life.

Hey these days we all want to be social influencers means youtuber.

Really?

And to make it happen, the good guys are doing this by dropping out of school. Why do you think that studying is preventing your dreams from succeeding? The problem is not here. Smart phones have been available in our hands ever since. Since then, we have started to consider useless people as our own ideals. And what they are saying now is like a line of signs for us. Hey, first look at what you think is your ideal. Whether he deserves to be your ideal. Studying never hinders your dreams but helps to turn your dreams into reality.

And besides, not all of us are ready to do everything. When I see one of them, I have to follow it and I think this is for me.

Just then we begin to move away from the success of our lives. Hey, I used to think like them that every thing is for every human being. And with that in mind, I started learning music. And I started learning guitar. Believe me, there was no shortage of trying again. But I will never be a singer. My throat is not good. In fact, I was not prepared for it. Then I thought I would be a motivational speaker.

Because I was made for it.

So learn to understand things. Never make anyone your ideal. If you want to discuss it, you can write a whole book.

Not without saying one thing.

Today we are so entangled in a false world that we are afraid to present ourselves in front of everyone

Can't believe it.

Today, we are moving away from real life and always prefer the false world. Today we are covering our real beauty through filters. Today we are exposing our body in front of everyone to get some like comments.

We always say that girls do extra quality makeup?

Once we think about why we do extra makeup?

For you

Because we have never loved a girl of black or black color.

When we gave them a place in our dreams. We didn't give them because we are just fairy tale books

I want to be bound by this. You believe that day you are more than the girl in the filter. Original

Like the girl outside the filter. That day the girl will stop giving filters.

You will be surprised that the world is involved in the life of each of us. One of our decisions has the power to change the world.

So if we can recognize the authentic things ourselves

People will start giving us authentic things even if they charge us a little more.

It's up to us what we do.

Because that's when we start to enter the real world from the false world. We will have no fear of losing or showing someone.

And we'll start to get better.

This is the beginning of a false world. By some lying people. And by our misunderstanding.

It is then possible to change. When we start to be educated. The importance of education will continue to grow in our society. I am not asking you to change the importance of education.

I say you educate yourself. If you can educate yourself. Here I am talking about educated in the true sense of the word. Then you will not set foot in the false world by your knowledge.

Only then can you pick up those who like to live in a false world.

This is how we start it.

TEN

MAKE YOUR OWN WORLD

We moved on to the last chapter to see. I never thought I would write so many pages. I don't know why I developed a relationship with you so I don't want to end it. Tears welled up in his eyes as he said good-bye. I have never told anyone so openly. Remember this as many times as you read this book. I am a more ordinary boy than you. Who dreams of transforming themselves like you. He wants to present himself to the society in a new way. And I want to create a meaning in the true sense of my life. I want to do something good for the people around me like you. By writing this book, I do not want to introduce myself as an author in front of you. I mean, I'm a form of you. I just want to remind you of that. I am your friend who wants to help you with your dreams. The words I will say now are the most valuable words in this book.

You may be wondering why I spelled the name of this chapter my own world?

So far I have talked about presenting myself in front of this world. Let's not create a world of our own. Where there will be only those whom we love and those who love us. Everything will be like the beach. Just like imagination.

So what you have to be prepared for is to face some of the toughest realities of this world.

You can. There will be some failures.

Let's go then

You will be able to accept this fact as soon as you go through life.

How was your day today

Are you ok

The number of people asking these words will gradually decrease as you get older. In fact, no matter what happens to you, it doesn't matter to anyone in the world. So you have to accept the hard truth first. You have to teach yourself something new every day. That means you have to remember every day that you learn something new every day. Because if you don't learn by yourself. Then why would people want to be in your world. You just have to be more discriminating with the help you render toward other people. It may take a long time, but you need to be patient. Change yourself.

The second hard truth we have to accept is that everyone we love from the heart will one day leave us. So we have to be ready all the time. I will never tell you to surrender yourself to others. I would say love every man as much as you do without humiliating yourself. That's all. Then you will never get in trouble.

Follow the rules I have told you to choose friends that you will make friends. They may not be with you for life. So you have to prepare yourself again. First make some rules of your life. That means exactly how many people around you do what you want to take. Suppose you decide that you will have only 10 friends in your life. If someone leaves you.

Wait for him for a while. After that time has passed, another new friend from the rules of choosing a friend in that place

Put it in its place. It's true that this sounds bad. If you can't do this you will never be good in life. So you have to do it.

Don't get involved in trivial matters unnecessarily. Suppose a fight is going on in the street and you can see from a distance whether it is possible for you to stop it. If not here's a new product just for you! Instead, call on those who can prevent it. Because you have to keep in your head that you are not a superhero. And if you keep seeing such minor incidents, you will continue to get hurt again and again.

You have to harden yourself a little.

You need to know how much social media you need. Stop using if not needed. Because it's behind you not being happy

Most. Suppose you watch a motivational video at night and think you will start everything from tomorrow in life. Suppose you are a little fat and you decide that tomorrow you will start running. How good is your decision. But tomorrow when you wake up in the morning you will see that a friend who is fatter than you has made a six pack body. The video of Motivation that you saw tomorrow will seem trivial to you and you will start to suffer from depression. You will not see for once that he has made his own six pack body using filters. But if you didn't open the Facebook app in that place, you would have finished your first race by now. So if you do not need to uninstall the apps. Where you are now or where you are working if you are in school or college. Wrong there

Stop making mistakes. And start using the good aspects there. And think about what you can do using them. He has your advantage. There is no point in catching mistakes here and there. Nowadays everyone is a motivational speaker on social media. So stop misunderstanding them. If you like a word or two or you think they are needed in your life. Then forget the rest with them. You may now feel that you have time. In fact, the least we have is time. So start paying the price of time. If you play games you are doing it wrong. That's where you do things to reach your goal. It benefits you. Do not listen to people at all. You are completely different from everyone else. So do the work that you do with so much love. As if this work is more than you

No one can do a good job. No one has ever done that before. It is very important to work every day. Because if you do not work, you will never be able to create a beautiful world of your own.

Nowadays there is a saying that you want our freedom. But remember that extra freedom always makes us reckless. So bind yourself to the rules and regulations. It will help you reach your goal. Stop chatting too much with friends. Read some good books in that place. When you have time, go out somewhere. You will get a chance to know yourself in the gap of work. Understand how much worse people are than you. How much do you need in the world. And then it will feel bad to waste your life in vain. I always think we should go outside so we can understand how insignificant we are compared to this world.

As a result, if we have the slightest bit of arrogance in our minds, it will be ruined.

Make yourself such that every person who is with you misses you the most when you leave them. They say I had a friend. Really very good.

But your life is successful. Only then will you find your real money. Never change yourself.

I am not surprised. I told you to change the whole book and in the last episode I told you not to change.

I am not asking you to change like that. You see, when we dream in life, our intention to do something is never bad. Let me explain more clearly

This means that if you want to be a good officer, first of all when you want to be a good officer, your intention is to sit in that chair.

People can do better all the time. But when we get that chair or fulfill that dream. Then we forget our real purpose and start self-fulfillment through that chair. Which is why we start going the wrong way. Fear of being caught begins to be feared in our minds. And then we forget to be good. But think once you have completed your dream. And your intentions remained the same. Then you could create a beautiful environment. A lot of people get love. That bold truth would have awakened in you. And you started to get better then.

Isn't it?

You will see that many people will give you a lot of trouble on the way of life, many times you will get many injuries. But forgive them. Because remember that many people will come into your life on the way to life, some of them will make you suffer a lot. And some people will teach you to love. Give some beautiful moments. So forget their bad aspects and move forward with these moments of those who gave you good moments. You will be much better. If you can forgive them. Then you will see that one day when they realize their mistake, they will love you the most. To them you will be no less than a superhero.

This is the world we have not come to live in forever. Then what is so angry and arrogant. There are so many people in the world if you start mixing with one every day then your life will be over. But there will be no people on earth. So what is the benefit of being angry at someone but forgetting him and becoming a new person

Interact with people.

Don't mix with some people who are limited all the time. Occasionally you will meet new people and they will help you to forget your past. You will be able to present yourself in a new way. It benefits you a lot.

And through these we can build a beautiful world. I want to build your hand. Let's all change the society in a beautiful little way. We may not be the richest people in the world. But I can be one of the ten people around us. Because it is in our hands.

Society really needs a good person like you so don't ruin yourself.

I don't want to go but I have to finish. Because everything has an end. To put it better, those who have a beginning also have an end. So I ended up here. This is my first book so I haven't experienced it that way. In the meantime, if I ever hurt you. Then forgive me. In fact I forgot to tell you my name is The MOMI or not it is to show my people. But you can call me Mominul. I haven't studied literature so I don't have much linguistic knowledge. If you make a mistake, you must forgive. And if you have any problems in life, you can definitely message me and I will try to solve them as a personal friend of yours. I want to give you the number. All right, you will do one thing. You will let me know by texting @mominul_amin. I will answer.

Stay well, stay healthy, take care of yourself

Mominul Amin

Printed by Libri Plureos GmbH in Hamburg, Germany